The Mind of Women

Gerard Roussel

Copyright Page

Index

Gerard Roussel

Gerard Roussel

Understanding the Feminine Mind

The female mind is a fascinating and complex field, full of nuances and particularities that have been the object of study and curiosity for centuries. To understand it, it is essential to recognize that there is not a single type of female mind; Each woman is a universe in herself, with thoughts, emotions and experiences that shape her uniquely. However, there are certain common patterns and characteristics that help us better understand how female psychology works and, ultimately, how we can support women to understand themselves.

From the beginning, it is crucial to emphasize that the female mind is neither simpler nor more complicated than the male mind; it just operates differently in some ways. These differences are neither universal nor rigid, but they help explain why women tend to experience the world in a particular way. One of the most influential factors in the way the female mind works is biology. Women's brains are structured in a way that allows them to be exceptionally skilled at emotional perception and empathy. This means that, in general, women tend to be more in tune with their own emotions and those of others. This ability to pick up and process emotional cues is one of the reasons why many women are so intuitive and emotionally connected to their surroundings.

But it's not all biology. The female mind is also deeply influenced by the society and culture in which it operates. From an early age, girls are socialized to be caregivers, to be in tune with the feelings of others, and to value cooperation over competition. These teachings, often unconscious, shape the way women think, feel and act. For example, many women learn to prioritize the needs of others over their own, which can lead them to develop a strong sense of responsibility and sometimes a tendency to neglect their own well-being.

The female mind is also very sensitive to social expectations. In many cultures, women are under pressure to conform to certain roles and norms, which can lead to internal conflict and affect their self-esteem.

For example, women are expected to be simultaneously successful in their careers, devoted mothers, and loving partners, all while maintaining an "ideal" physical appearance. This burden of expectations can be overwhelming and can lead women to question themselves and feel like they are never doing enough. However, it is important to recognize that these expectations are social constructions, not absolute truths, and that each woman has the right to define her own path.

Another key aspect of the female mind is its ability to handle multiple tasks and responsibilities at the same time. Many women have an amazing ability to balance their personal, professional and social lives, which requires a great deal of mental and emotional energy. This ability to multitask is often seen as a strength, but it can also be a source of stress and burnout. It is vital that women learn to recognize when they are taking on too much and set healthy boundaries to protect their well-being.

The hormonal cycle also plays an important role in women's lives and how they experience the world. Hormonal fluctuations that occur throughout the menstrual cycle can affect mood, energy, and emotional perception. Although these changes are completely normal, they can be disconcerting if not well understood. It is essential that women have access to clear and accurate information about how their bodies and minds are connected, so they can navigate these changes with greater confidence and less anxiety.

An often underrated aspect of the female mind is its resilience. Throughout history, women have faced countless challenges, from gender inequalities to restrictive social expectations. However, they have demonstrated an incredible ability to adapt, overcome adversity and move forward. This resilience is not just a matter of willpower, but also of women's ability to support each other, find creative solutions to problems, and maintain a long-term vision even in difficult times.

Finally, it is important to highlight that understanding the female mind is not only an intellectual exercise, but a tool to promote well-being and self-acceptance. By better understanding how they think and feel, women can learn to be kinder to themselves, recognize their own patterns of thinking and behavior, and make more conscious decisions about their lives. Furthermore, this understanding can help create a more empathetic and supportive world, where differences are celebrated and women feel valued and understood in all their complexity.

In short, the female mind is a rich and varied landscape, shaped by biology, culture, personal experiences, and social expectations. Although every woman is unique, there are commonalities that allow us to offer a deeper understanding of how they think and feel. By exploring these topics with an open mind and an empathetic heart, we can support women on their journey toward self-acceptance and well-being, helping them live fuller, more satisfying lives.

Female Brain vs. Male Brain

The brain is one of the most fascinating and complex structures in the human body, and although the brains of men and women are more similar than they are different, there are certain distinctions that can influence how each gender perceives the world, processes information and reacts to different situations. It is important to clarify from the beginning that these differences do not imply superiority or inferiority of one gender over the other; rather, they help us better understand the natural variations in thinking and behavior between women and men.

One of the most frequently mentioned differences between female and male brains lies in how different regions of the brain are connected. In general, studies have shown that the female brain tends to have more connections between the left and right hemispheres, while in men, the connections tend to be stronger within each hemisphere. This means that women, on average, tend to better integrate emotional information (right hemisphere) with logical and verbal information (left hemisphere). As a result, women often have a remarkable ability to read and understand the emotions of both their own and others, allowing them to be more empathetic and attuned to interpersonal relationships.

On the other hand, the male brain is usually more specialized, with a greater ability to focus on specific tasks and process information in a more linear way. This difference may explain why men sometimes prefer to approach a problem directly and focused, while women may consider multiple perspectives and emotional factors before making a decision. In everyday situations, this can be reflected in how genders handle conflict or solve problems: women might want to discuss feelings and explore various options, while men might lean toward a quick and efficient solution.

Brain size is another aspect that is often discussed, although it is important not to misinterpret this information. On average, the male brain is slightly larger than the female brain. However, this does not mean that men are more intelligent; Brain size is not directly related to intellectual capacity. In fact, the density of neurons and the efficiency of connections are more important than size. In women, the brain may be smaller in terms of volume, but it is often denser in some key regions, allowing them to process information quickly and efficiently.

Another point of interest is how the male and female brains react to stress. Research suggests that women tend to activate more areas of the brain related to emotion and memory when faced with stressful situations. This could explain why women often remember the emotional details of stressful events and tend to process stress through conversation and social support. In contrast, men may show a more physical response to stress, activating areas of the brain that prepare the body for a fight or flight response. This difference could be why men sometimes prefer to deal with stress through physical activity or temporary isolation.

Language is another area where the brains of men and women can differ. Women tend to have greater verbal ability from an early age, which is reflected in greater verbal fluency and an ability to express feelings with words. This doesn't mean that men can't be good communicators, but rather that, on average, women tend to have an advantage in verbal and emotional communication. This difference is due, in part, to the fact that women tend to use both hemispheres of the brain when processing language, while men tend to primarily use the left hemisphere.

However, it is important to note that these differences are generalizations and do not apply to everyone. The neuroplasticity of the brain, or its ability to change and adapt, means that each person, regardless of their gender, can develop skills and abilities based on their experiences and environment. Furthermore, many of these differences are influenced by cultural and social factors that shape the way men and women are educated and behave.

In terms of emotions, women tend to be more expressive and experience a wider range of emotions compared to men. This doesn't mean that men don't feel emotions intensely, but rather that culturally they have often been taught not to express them so openly. The female brain has more mirror neurons, which are cells that help us understand and empathize with the feelings of others, which may explain why women are often more sensitive to the emotions of those around them.

Finally, it is essential to remember that while differences between male and female brains can influence certain behaviors, these differences do not determine a person's destiny. Each individual is unique, with a brain that shapes and adapts based on his or her experiences, education, and environment. Understanding these differences can help us improve communication and cooperation between men and women, recognizing and valuing the strengths that each brings to the table.

In short, the brains of men and women have some differences in their structure and functioning, but these variations do not make one better or worse than the other. Instead of focusing on the differences, it is more useful to see how these variations can complement and enrich our interactions. By better understanding how the female brain works compared to the male, we can appreciate the diversity of thoughts, emotions and approaches that each gender brings to the world, and learn to work together more harmoniously and effectively.

Women and Emotions

Emotions are an essential part of the human experience, and for many women, they are a powerful force that influences almost every aspect of their life. Understanding how women experience and manage emotions is key to understanding them better, since, although all human beings have emotions, women often experience them in a more intense and complex way. This intensity is not a sign of weakness or instability, but rather a manifestation of the deep connection that many women have with their feelings and with the people around them.

From a young age, girls are often encouraged to express their emotions, talk about how they feel, and connect emotionally with others. This is in contrast to many children, who are often taught to suppress their feelings or not show vulnerability. As a result, women often develop greater emotional fluidity, meaning they can identify, label, and communicate their emotions more easily. This ability to articulate feelings is one of the reasons why women often seek emotional support in times of stress or conflict, turning to friends, family, or even writing to process what they feel.

But women's relationship with emotions is not always easy. In a society that often underestimates or devalues emotions, women can feel caught between the need to express their feelings and the pressure to be "strong" or "rational." This tension can lead to an emotional turmoil in which women feel guilty for having strong emotions or showing vulnerability. However, it is important to remember that emotions are not something to be repressed or ignored; They are a vital part of what makes us human and connect us to our experiences and to others.

A fascinating aspect of how women experience emotions is their ability to feel multiple emotions at the same time. For example, a woman may feel happy about a friend's success while simultaneously feeling envious of that same achievement. This ability to manage complex and sometimes contradictory emotions reflects women's emotional depth and their ability to navigate the complicated emotional landscape of everyday life. However, this emotional wealth can also be exhausting, and without the right tools to manage it, it can lead to stress, anxiety, or even depression.

The hormonal cycle also plays a crucial role in women's emotional experience. Throughout the month, fluctuations in the levels of hormones such as estrogen and progesterone can influence mood and emotional sensitivity. Many women experience changes in their energy level, how they perceive everyday events, and their emotional reactivity depending on what phase of their cycle they are in. During premenstruation, for example, some women may feel more irritable, sensitive or sad for no apparent reason. Understanding this connection between hormones and emotions can help women be more compassionate with themselves and recognize that these feelings are natural and temporary.

Another important characteristic of women's relationship with emotions is their tendency to care for and nurture others. Many women find a deep sense of purpose in emotionally supporting their loved ones, which can be a source of satisfaction and happiness. However, this focus on others can also lead to neglecting your own emotional needs. It's common for women to try so hard to make sure everyone around them is okay that they forget to take care of their own emotional well-being. Learning to find a balance between giving and receiving emotional support is crucial to maintaining positive mental health.

Empathy is another cornerstone in the emotional life of many women. This ability to put yourself in another person's shoes and feel what they feel is a powerful skill that can strengthen relationships and create deep connections. Women are often adept at reading body language, facial expressions, and tones of voice, allowing them to pick up on others' emotions even when they are not expressed verbally. This empathy can be a gift, but it can also be exhausting, especially if a woman feels overwhelmed by the emotional problems of those around her. This is where the importance of self-care and the need to set emotional boundaries to protect her own mental health comes into play.

Throughout life, women develop an incredible variety of strategies to manage their emotions. Some turn to exercise, meditation, or writing as ways to process what they feel. Others seek support from close friends or therapy to talk about their emotional experiences. The important thing is that each woman finds what works best for her and gives herself permission to experience and express her emotions in a healthy way. There is no "right" or "wrong" way to feel; What matters is that women learn to be kind to themselves and treat their emotions with the respect and attention they deserve.

The role of culture and society is also fundamental in how women manage their emotions. In many cultures, women are expected to be the emotional caregivers, which can create additional pressure to remain calm and composed at all times. However, it is important to remember that emotions are natural and necessary, and that it is unrealistic or healthy to try to suppress or ignore them. Women should feel that they have the right to express their emotions, whether they are joy, sadness, anger or fear, without fear of being judged or rejected.

Ultimately, women's relationship with emotions is a central aspect of their identity and well-being. By learning to understand and accept their emotions, women can live fuller, more authentic lives. This process of self-understanding and acceptance is a continuous journey, full of challenges and discoveries, but also growth and empowerment. Emotions are not an enemy to overcome, but an ally on the path to a rich and meaningful life.

In short, emotions play a crucial role in women's lives, shaping their experiences and relationships in deep and meaningful ways. Although they can be overwhelming at times, emotions are also a source of strength, empathy, and connection. By better understanding how women experience and manage their emotions, we can support women on their path to self-awareness and emotional well-being, helping them live with greater balance and happiness.

The Hormonal Cycle and its Psychological Impact

The hormonal cycle is a fundamental part of many women's lives, and although it is often talked about in physical terms, its impact goes far beyond bodily symptoms. The hormonal fluctuations that occur throughout the menstrual cycle have a profound effect on a woman's mood, energy, and the way she experiences the world. Understanding how these hormones affect the female mind is key to helping women navigate these changes with greater awareness and control.

To start, it's helpful to understand that the menstrual cycle is not just a monthly event; It is a continuous process that lasts approximately 28 days, although it can vary from one woman to another. During this time, levels of different hormones, such as estrogen, progesterone, and testosterone, rise and fall, affecting the body and mind in subtle and not-so-subtle ways. Each phase of the cycle has specific characteristics that influence how a woman feels emotionally, mentally and physically.

The first phase of the cycle, known as the follicular phase, begins with the first day of menstruation. During this time, estrogen levels begin to rise, which can bring a feeling of renewal and energy. Many women feel more optimistic and motivated in this phase, with greater mental clarity and an improved ability to concentrate. It is a time when emotions tend to be more stable, and women may feel more sociable and open to new experiences.

As estrogen continues to rise, the body prepares for ovulation, which occurs mid-cycle. Ovulation is a brief but powerful event in which estrogen levels peak, which can lead to an increase in energy, sexual desire, and confidence. Many women feel more confident and attractive during ovulation, which can influence how they interact with others and make decisions. This is a time when the female mind may be particularly focused on relationships and connection with others.

After ovulation, the body enters the luteal phase, where estrogen levels begin to drop and progesterone takes over. Progesterone is a hormone that has a calming effect on the body and mind, which can make women feel more relaxed and less inclined to action. However, as the luteal phase progresses, many women begin to experience premenstrual symptoms, such as irritability, fatigue, and mood swings. These symptoms, often grouped under the term Premenstrual Syndrome (PMS), are the result of a drop in hormone levels and can make women feel more sensitive or emotionally vulnerable.

The psychological impact of these hormonal changes can be significant. During the premenstrual phase, some women may feel more anxious or depressed, even if there is no obvious reason for this. Emotional sensitivity increases, and what would normally be a minor annoyance can seem overwhelming. It is common for women to feel more introspective or need more time alone to process their emotions during this phase. It's important for women to recognize these feelings as a natural part of the cycle and not judge themselves for feeling "different" these days.

The hormonal cycle not only affects mood, but also perception and thinking. For example, during the premenstrual phase, some women may notice that their mind tends to focus more on problems or challenges, while during the follicular phase, they may feel more creative and optimistic. This fluctuation in focus and perspective is natural, and it can be helpful for women to plan their activities based on the phase they are in. For example, the days after menstruation may be a good time to start new projects or activities that require a lot of energy, while the premenstrual phase could be more suitable for reflection and rest.

Another important aspect to consider is how these hormonal fluctuations can influence self-esteem and body image. During the luteal phase, when the body retains more fluids and swelling may occur, some women may feel less comfortable with their physical appearance, which can affect their confidence. It is crucial for women to be aware that these feelings are temporary and do not reflect their true value or beauty.

Accepting that the body and mind are constantly changing throughout the cycle can help reduce self-criticism and encourage a more compassionate attitude toward oneself.

Although the hormonal cycle is a normal part of women's lives, it can be challenging to manage its emotional effects, especially in a world that often does not take these natural variations into account. Women sometimes feel pressure to "get over" their feelings or maintain consistent performance, no matter what phase of the cycle they are in. However, it is important for women to listen to their bodies and respect their emotional and physical needs during each phase of the cycle. This could mean taking a break when they feel overwhelmed, or taking advantage of high-energy moments to make progress on their goals.

Ultimately, understanding the hormonal cycle and its psychological impact allows women to become more aware of how their bodies and minds are interconnected. By recognizing patterns in their emotions and behaviors throughout the cycle, women can better anticipate and manage emotional challenges that may arise. This awareness can also empower them to make more informed decisions about their health and well-being, from planning their daily activities to how they relate to others.

In summary, the hormonal cycle has a significant impact on the emotional and psychological lives of women. Fluctuations in levels of estrogen, progesterone and other hormones not only affect the body, but also the mind, influencing how women feel, think and behave throughout the month. By better understanding these changes, women can learn to work with their cycle rather than fight it, allowing them to live with greater balance and well-being. The key is self-understanding and self-acceptance, recognizing that emotional ups and downs are a natural part of life and that, with the right tools, they can be managed effectively.

Female Self-Esteem

Self-esteem is the way we value ourselves and feel about ourselves, and for women, this self-worth can be a particularly complex issue. From a young age, women are faced with a barrage of messages about how they should look, behave and act, which can profoundly influence how they perceive themselves. Female self-esteem is not only related to physical appearance, but also to confidence in her abilities, her ability to make decisions, and her sense of value in the world.

One of the main challenges to female self-esteem is social pressure to meet certain beauty standards. Women are often bombarded with images of "perfect" bodies in the media, which can lead to constant comparisons and, in many cases, dissatisfaction with their own appearance. This pressure is not just limited to the body; It also covers how a woman should dress, speak and behave. The problem with these standards is that they are unattainable for most and can make women feel inadequate or not good enough.

It is essential that women learn to challenge these unrealistic expectations and develop a positive body image. The key is to recognize that each body is unique and that there is no single way to be beautiful. Accepting and loving one's body as it is, with its imperfections and uniqueness, is a crucial step in building strong self-esteem. This doesn't mean that a woman shouldn't take care of herself or make changes if she wants, but those changes should come from a place of self-love and not an attempt to meet the expectations of others.

Female self-esteem is also deeply linked to self-confidence, which is the belief in one's own ability to face challenges and succeed. Women can often doubt themselves and underestimate their abilities, especially in environments where they feel judged or compared to others. This lack of confidence can be debilitating, preventing a woman from pursuing her goals or making important decisions. It is common for women to face so-called "imposter syndrome," where they feel that they are not competent enough or that they do not deserve their achievements, even when they have clear evidence to the contrary.

To overcome these doubts, it is essential that women recognize and celebrate their achievements, no matter how small. Every victory, whether personal or professional, is a reminder of your ability and worth. It is also helpful for women to surround themselves with people who support and encourage them, rather than those who criticize or put them down. Positive feedback and support from friends, family or mentors can help boost self-confidence and self-esteem, providing a counterbalance to internal doubts.

Another important aspect of female self-esteem is the ability to set and maintain healthy boundaries. Women often feel the need to please others, whether in their personal relationships, at work, or in society in general. This desire to please can lead to excessive self-demand and the sacrifice of one's own needs and desires. However, learning to say "no" and prioritize your own well-being is essential to maintaining healthy self-esteem. Setting boundaries is not selfish; It is a form of self-care that allows women to protect their energy and focus on what is really important to them.

Self-esteem is also influenced by how a woman handles failure and criticism. It's natural to make mistakes or fail to meet expectations at some point, but how she deals with these challenges can have a lasting impact on her self-esteem. Women who have strong self-esteem tend to view failures as learning opportunities rather than a reflection of their worth. They learn to accept constructive criticism without letting it affect their sense of self. This doesn't mean ignoring criticism, but rather processing it so they can grow and improve without losing confidence in who they are.

In today's society, where social media plays such an important role, it is easy to fall into the trap of seeking external validation. Likes, positive comments, and approval from others may seem like a reflection of one's self-worth, but basing self-esteem on external validation is dangerous. True self-esteem must come from within, based on a solid sense of self-worth that does not depend on what others think or say. This requires women to know themselves deeply, to understand their values, strengths and weaknesses, and to accept themselves completely, with all their flaws and virtues.

The path to strong, healthy self-esteem is not easy, and it can be full of ups and downs. However, it is a journey worth taking, as positive self-esteem is essential to living a full and satisfying life. Women who have high self-esteem are not only happier, but they are also better equipped to face life's challenges, make important decisions, and build healthy, meaningful relationships. Additionally, strong self-esteem allows women to be authentic and live by their own values, rather than trying to meet the expectations of others.

It is important to remember that self-esteem is not a static state; It is something that can grow and strengthen over time. Women can work on their self-esteem in many ways, from practicing self-care and self-compassion to challenging negative thoughts and surrounding themselves with supportive people. It is also helpful for women to seek out activities and hobbies that make them feel fulfilled and satisfied, as these can help reinforce their sense of worth and competence.

In short, female self-esteem is a crucial aspect of emotional and mental well-being. Although many women face challenges on their path to healthy self-esteem, it is possible to overcome these obstacles and develop a strong sense of self-worth. By learning to love and accept their own bodies, celebrate their achievements, set healthy boundaries, handle failure constructively, and seek internal rather than external validation, women can build strong self-esteem that empowers them to live full and fulfilling lives. authentic. Self-esteem is not just a goal to achieve, but a continuous journey of self-knowledge, growth and self-love.

Women and Interpersonal Relationships

Interpersonal relationships are a vital part of anyone's life, but for many women, these connections hold a special place in their emotional and social world. Relationships with family, friends, partners, and co-workers are fundamental to women's well-being, as they often find in them a source of support, love, and validation. However, relationships can also be challenging, requiring time, energy, and sometimes a great deal of patience and understanding.

From a young age, women tend to develop strong social and emotional skills. They are encouraged to be empathetic, care for others, and maintain harmony in their relationships. These skills are invaluable in creating and maintaining deep, meaningful connections, but they can also lead women to prioritize the needs of others over their own. This focus on care and attention to others is beautiful, but it can also be exhausting if not balanced with self-care and setting healthy boundaries.

One of the most notable characteristics of female interpersonal relationships is the importance of emotional support. Women often turn to their friends, sisters, or mothers to share their feelings, vent, and seek advice. These conversations not only strengthen the bonds between them, but also provide a safe space to express emotions and solve problems. The ability to communicate openly and honestly is one of the reasons why relationships between women can be so deep and long-lasting. However, this emotional exchange can also be a double-edged sword, as women can become overly dependent on these relationships for their emotional well-being.

The balance between giving and receiving support is key in any relationship. Sometimes women can feel obligated to be the "rock" in their relationships, always willing to listen and provide help, even when they themselves are going through difficult times. This caregiver role can be rewarding, but it can also lead to emotional exhaustion if not handled properly. It is crucial that women learn to ask for help when they need it and to allow others to take care of them from time to time. Mutual support is essential to maintaining healthy and sustainable long-term relationships.

Romantic relationships are another central aspect of many women's lives, and they can be both a source of great happiness and stress. The way women approach romantic relationships is often influenced by a combination of cultural, familial, and personal factors. Some women may feel pressure to find a partner and settle down, while others seek a relationship that will allow them to grow and evolve as individuals. In both cases, it's important for women to feel valued and respected in their relationships, and that these connections bring them more joy than pain.

In romantic relationships, communication is essential. Sometimes women may have unexpressed expectations or assume that their partner understands their needs without them having to say so. However, for a relationship to work well, it is necessary to talk openly about what is desired and expected. This not only strengthens the relationship, but also avoids long-term misunderstandings and resentments. Women who can communicate their needs clearly and assertively are more likely to experience healthy, satisfying relationships.

Conflicts are an inevitable part of any relationship, whether romantic, friendly, or family. How these conflicts are handled can determine the quality and duration of the relationship. Many women tend to avoid conflict to keep the peace, but this strategy can lead to bigger problems in the future. Instead of avoiding conflict, it is more useful to approach it constructively, seeking solutions that benefit both parties. Learning to resolve disagreements respectfully and productively is a valuable skill that can improve the quality of all interpersonal relationships.

Family relationships also play an important role in women's lives. Women are often the ones who maintain the bond between family members, organizing gatherings, caring for aging parents, and being the glue that holds everyone together. Although these responsibilities can be rewarding, they can also be a burden if they are not shared equally. It is important for women to learn to delegate and ask for help when necessary, so as not to feel overwhelmed by family demands.

In the workplace, interpersonal relationships are also essential. Women often form support networks with colleagues that can be invaluable for professional development and emotional well-being. However, the work environment can also be a space where relationships become complicated, especially if there is competition or conflict. Here, clear communication, mutual respect, and the ability to manage stress are essential to maintaining healthy working relationships. Additionally, it is important that women feel empowered to defend their rights and opinions at work, without fear of reprisals or lawsuits.

Setting limits is a recurring theme in all interpersonal relationships. Women often have a tendency to want to be there for everyone, which can lead to emotional and physical overload. Learning to say "no" when necessary, and to protect personal time and energy, is essential to maintaining mental and emotional health. This does not mean being selfish, but recognizing that in order to take care of others, you must first take care of yourself.

Finally, it is important for women to remember that not all relationships are healthy or beneficial. Sometimes it is necessary to distance yourself from people who are toxic or who do not respect your boundaries and needs. This can be difficult, especially if it is a close relationship, but it is crucial for long-term well-being. Women deserve to be surrounded by people who value them, respect them, and support them in their personal and emotional growth.

In short, interpersonal relationships are an essential part of women's lives and can be a source of great joy and satisfaction. However, they also require effort, communication, and the ability to manage conflict and set boundaries. By learning to balance giving and receiving support, communicating effectively, and protecting their own well-being, women can build healthy, meaningful relationships that enrich their lives. The connections they form with others not only provide them with companionship and love, but also help them grow as people, strengthening their self-esteem and their sense of purpose in the world.

The Role of Culture in Female Psychology

Culture is a powerful force that influences almost every aspect of our lives, and for women, its impact on psychology is particularly profound. From childhood, women are shaped by the norms, values, and expectations of the culture in which they live, which affects the way they think, feel, and behave. These cultural influences not only define what it means to be a woman in a society, but they also have an impact on how women view the world and themselves. Understanding how culture shapes female psychology is crucial to understanding women's personal development, relationships, and emotional well-being.

Each culture has its own ideas about what is appropriate or expected for women. In many societies, girls are taught from a young age to be kind, compassionate, and care for others. These qualities are valued and encouraged, while other behaviors, such as assertiveness or independence, may be less encouraged or even discouraged. As a result, many women grow up feeling that their value is tied to their ability to please others or to fulfill certain traditional roles, such as being mothers or wives.

This process of cultural socialization not only affects external behavior, but also the internal world of women. Cultural expectations can influence how a woman feels about herself, often leading her to internalize ideas about what she should be and how she should act. For example, in cultures where physical appearance is highly valued, women may feel constant pressure to look a certain way, which can affect their self-esteem and emotional well-being. Similarly, in societies where women are expected to be submissive or dependent, those who wish to live more independently may face internal and external conflicts when trying to reconcile their personal desires with cultural expectations.

The influence of culture on female psychology also manifests itself in the way women manage their emotions and relationships. In some cultures, women are expected to be emotional caregivers, always willing to listen and support others, while their own emotional needs may be overlooked. This expectation can lead women to develop a strong sense of responsibility toward the feelings of others, often at the expense of their own well-being. Learning to balance this cultural expectation with self-care is a challenge that many women face throughout their lives.

In addition to expectations about behavior and emotions, culture also influences the opportunities women have to grow and develop. In many cultures, women have had less access to education, employment, and other opportunities than men, which has limited their ability to reach their full potential. Although these barriers are decreasing in many parts of the world, the effects of centuries of inequality are still felt, and many women continue to face obstacles to advancing their careers or achieving their personal goals.

It is important to recognize that culture is not monolithic; Within each society, there are subcultures and variations that can offer different models and expectations for women. For example, within the same community, there may be women who adhere to traditional roles and others who challenge those norms, creating a diversity of experiences and perspectives. This cultural diversity can be a source of strength and resilience for women, offering them different paths and opportunities to define their own identities.

Globalization has also expanded cultural influences on female psychology, exposing women to ideas and values from different parts of the world. This can be both positive and negative. On the one hand, women can find inspiration and support in global movements for gender equality and women's rights. On the other hand, exposure to different cultures and standards can lead to confusion or internal conflict, especially if the values of your home culture differ from those found elsewhere.

Throughout history, women have used culture as a tool for self-expression and empowerment. Art, literature, music, and other forms of cultural expression have allowed women to share their stories, explore their identity, and challenge established norms. Through these cultural expressions, women have been able to find their voice and claim their place in society, often in ways that transcend the limitations imposed by their culture.

As culture evolves, so does female psychology. Changes in cultural norms and values can open up new possibilities for women, allowing them to explore different roles and ways of life that were not available before. However, these changes can also create tensions, as women must navigate between traditional expectations and new opportunities. This tension can be a source of stress, but also of personal growth, as women redefine what it means to be a woman in their time and place.

In short, culture plays a central role in the formation of female psychology. Cultural norms, values, and expectations influence how women see themselves, how they manage their emotions and relationships, and what opportunities they have to grow and develop. Although culture can be a source of pressure and limitation, it can also be a source of strength and empowerment. By understanding how culture shapes their psychology, women can find ways to live more authentically and fully, challenging limiting expectations and taking advantage of the opportunities their world offers them. The key is to recognize cultural influence, reflect on it, and consciously decide how to integrate it into their lives in a way that allows them to flourish and truly be themselves.

Fear and Anxiety in Women

Fear and anxiety are natural human emotions that we all experience at some point in our lives. However, for many women, these emotions can play a more prominent and persistent role, affecting their emotional well-being and quality of life. Understanding how fear and anxiety manifest in women's lives, and how these emotions are influenced by biological, psychological, and social factors, is essential to addressing these challenges and promoting more balanced mental health.

Fear is an instinctive response that helps us protect ourselves from danger. When we face a threat, our body activates the "fight or flight" system, preparing us to face danger or escape from it. This response is essential for our survival, but in the modern world, where threats are not always physical, fear can become disproportionate or misdirected. For women, certain fears may be particularly common due to life experiences and cultural expectations. For example, fear of violence, harassment, or discrimination may be more pronounced due to the reality that these threats are more frequent in women's lives.

Anxiety, on the other hand, is a more persistent response that often manifests as constant worry, nervousness, or a general feeling of unease. While fear is a response to a specific, imminent threat, anxiety is more diffuse and may be related to worries about the future or the perception of having no control over situations. Women tend to experience anxiety more frequently than men, and this may be related to a combination of hormonal, social, and psychological factors.

One of the biological factors that influence female anxiety is the hormonal cycle. Hormonal fluctuations during the menstrual cycle, pregnancy, and menopause can affect mood and increase susceptibility to anxiety. During menstruation, for example, estrogen and progesterone levels fluctuate, which can cause changes in brain chemistry and increase anxiety. Similarly, pregnancy and menopause are periods of major hormonal changes that can trigger or intensify feelings of anxiety in some women.

In addition to biological factors, social and cultural expectations also play a crucial role in how women experience fear and anxiety. From a young age, women are often socialized to be careful, to avoid risks, and to worry about the safety of others. These expectations can lead women to internalize a greater sense of vulnerability or responsibility, which in turn can increase their predisposition to anxiety. For example, women may feel constant pressure to fulfill multiple roles, such as being good mothers, wives, daughters, and professionals, which can cause considerable stress and anxiety.

Fear of failure or not living up to expectations is another factor that can contribute to anxiety in women. In a society where women are expected to be successful in all areas of their lives, from their career to their personal life, the pressure to live up to these ideals can be overwhelming. This pressure can lead to a cycle of worry and self-criticism, where women constantly feel anxious about not doing enough or being good enough. This type of anxiety, which is linked to self-demand and perfectionism, is common in many women and can affect both their mental health and their general well-being.

Fear and anxiety can also be related to past experiences of trauma or abuse. Women who have experienced traumatic situations, such as domestic violence, sexual abuse, or stalking, may develop chronic anxiety as a result of these experiences. This type of anxiety, which often manifests itself in the form of post-traumatic stress disorder (PTSD), can be debilitating and require specialized treatment. It is important for women who have gone through these experiences to seek support and therapy, as appropriate treatment can help relieve anxiety and improve their quality of life.

Fortunately, there are many effective strategies for managing fear and anxiety in women's lives. One of the most important is learning to recognize and challenge anxious thoughts. Anxiety is often fueled by catastrophic thoughts or the tendency to imagine the worst. Identifying these thoughts and replacing them with more realistic and balanced thoughts can help reduce anxiety. It is also helpful to practice relaxation techniques, such as deep breathing, meditation, or yoga, which can calm the nervous system and decrease the anxiety response.

Self-care also plays a crucial role in managing fear and anxiety. For many women, the simple act of taking care of themselves, whether through healthy eating, regular exercise, or adequate rest, can make a big difference in their anxiety level. Additionally, it's important for women to give themselves permission to rest and relax, especially in a culture that values constant productivity. Time dedicated to pleasant and relaxing activities is not a luxury, but a necessity to maintain emotional balance.

Social connection is another key factor in reducing fear and anxiety. Talking to friends, family, or a therapist about what you are feeling can ease the emotional burden and provide an outside perspective that can be very helpful. Women tend to be good at building support networks, and tapping into these networks can be a powerful way to manage anxiety. Sharing experiences and listening to other women facing similar challenges can help normalize feelings of anxiety and find practical solutions.

In some cases, anxiety may be severe enough to require medical intervention. Treatments such as cognitive behavioral therapy (CBT) and anti-anxiety medications have been shown to be effective for many women who struggle with anxiety. CBT, in particular, helps people identify and change negative thought patterns that contribute to anxiety, while medications can be helpful in managing symptoms in the short term. It is important for women to speak with a mental health professional to determine the best approach for their specific situation.

In short, fear and anxiety are common emotions that can have a significant impact on women's lives. These emotions are influenced by a combination of biological, social, and psychological factors, and can manifest in different ways at different times in life. However, with the right strategies and the necessary support, it is possible to manage fear and anxiety effectively, reducing its impact and allowing women to live more balanced and satisfying lives. Understanding and addressing these emotions is a crucial step toward better mental health and overall well-being.

Women at Work

The workplace has been a terrain of struggle and constant evolution for women. Throughout history, the role of women at work has changed dramatically, from a time when opportunities were limited and largely restricted to the home, to the present, where women are present in almost all fields. professionals, challenging stereotypes and breaking barriers. However, despite progress, many women continue to face unique challenges in the workplace. Understanding these challenges, as well as the strengths and strategies women employ to overcome them, is essential to promoting equity and success at work.

One of the most significant transformations in the role of women at work is the increasing female participation in the workforce. In decades past, women were often expected to primarily do household chores and care for the family, while men were the primary economic providers. However, with social and economic changes, more and more women have entered the workforce, seeking not only economic independence, but also personal and professional fulfillment. This participation has been fundamental to economic growth and has helped redefine what it means to be a working woman in modern society.

Despite these advances, women in the workplace still face significant obstacles. One of the most persistent is the gender pay gap. In many countries, women still earn less than men for doing the same work. This pay disparity not only reflects economic injustice, but is also an indicator of the inequalities of power and valuation that still exist in many work environments. The fight for equal pay is one of the main demands of the feminist movement and a crucial step towards equality at work.

Another major challenge for women at work is the "glass ceiling." This term refers to the invisible barriers that prevent women from advancing to leadership and decision-making positions in their careers. Although many women manage to enter and excel in their professions, they often find promotion to the highest levels of management more difficult to achieve.

These barriers may be the result of unconscious biases, lack of support networks, or the expectation that women must choose between family and career. As a result, women are underrepresented in leadership positions, perpetuating gender inequality in the workplace.

Work-life balance is another crucial aspect of a woman's experience at work. Many women feel pressure to meet expectations in both their career and personal lives, which can lead to significant emotional and physical drain. Society often expects women to be mothers and caregivers as well as successful workers, creating a double burden. Although men also face challenges in this area, the pressure to balance both worlds is particularly intense for women, which can sometimes lead to feelings of guilt or inadequacy.

Workplace policies that support work-life balance are critical to helping women overcome these challenges. Maternity and paternity leave, flexible working, and accessible childcare are examples of measures that can make a big difference. In workplaces where these policies are implemented, women have more opportunities to advance their careers without having to sacrifice their personal lives. Furthermore, these policies not only benefit women, but also promote a more equitable and fair work environment for all employees.

In addition to structural challenges, women at work also face cultural and psychological barriers. Gender norms and stereotypes often influence how women are perceived at work. For example, women who are assertive and ambitious may be viewed negatively, while those same behaviors in men are valued as signs of leadership. This "double standard" can make women hesitate to express their opinions or aspire to leadership positions, for fear of being judged or marginalized.

To counter these challenges, many women have developed skills and strategies that allow them to navigate the work environment successfully. Building support networks is one of the most powerful tools available to women at work. Mentoring networks, both formal and informal, can provide guidance, support, and professional development opportunities. Women who support each other and form alliances in the workplace can collectively challenge the barriers they face, promoting a more inclusive and equitable work environment.

Resilience is another key characteristic that many women have developed in response to workplace challenges. The ability to bounce back from setbacks, learn from experiences, and continue moving forward is essential to success in any career. Women who have overcome significant obstacles often demonstrate great strength and determination, which not only allows them to advance their own careers, but also inspires others to keep going.

Furthermore, diversity and inclusion are increasingly recognized as crucial factors for organizational success. Companies that value gender diversity and promote inclusion tend to be more innovative, competitive and successful. Women bring different perspectives, skills, and approaches to the workplace, which can enrich decision-making and improve organizational performance. For this reason, many organizations are implementing initiatives to promote gender equality, reduce the pay gap, and support the professional development of women.

In short, women's experience at work is complex and multifaceted. Although significant progress has been made in gender equality in the workplace, significant challenges remain to be addressed. Women continue to face barriers such as the wage gap, the glass ceiling, and the pressure to balance work and personal life. However, through resilience, mutual support, and the promotion of inclusive policies, women are transforming the workplace and paving the way for future generations. Women's success at work not only benefits themselves, but also enriches organizations and society as a whole, promoting a more just and equitable future for all.

Maternity

Motherhood is a transformative experience that touches every aspect of a woman's life. It is a journey full of intense emotions, deep responsibilities, and significant changes in both body and mind. Although motherhood is one of the most natural and universal experiences, it is also one of the most complex and challenging. For many women, becoming a mother not only means caring for a child, but also redefining themselves, finding a new balance in life, and facing both internal and external expectations that can be overwhelming.

The beginning of motherhood, for many women, is marked by pregnancy, a period of profound physical and emotional changes. During these months, a woman's body adapts to nourish and protect the developing baby. These changes can be exciting and amazing, but they can also be challenging. The hormones circulating through the body not only affect the physique, but also the mood, which can lead to feelings of joy, anxiety, or even sadness. The anticipation of the baby's arrival brings with it a flood of emotions, from joy and excitement to fear and uncertainty.

One of the most powerful aspects of motherhood is the emotional bond that forms between a mother and her child. This bond begins during pregnancy and is strengthened with the birth and daily care of the baby. It is a connection that is deeply rooted in biology, but also in emotional experience. Many women describe this bond as unconditional love, a feeling of protection and total dedication that they have never experienced before. However, the process of forming this bond can be different for each woman, and it doesn't always happen right away. Some mothers feel connected to their baby from the first moment, while others need time to adapt to her new role and establish that connection.

Motherhood also brings with it a sense of responsibility that can be overwhelming. Suddenly, a woman finds herself in the position of being the primary caregiver for a completely dependent being. This sense of responsibility can fill mothers with an intense desire to do everything possible to ensure the well-being of their child. However, it can also generate anxiety and pressure. Worrying about doing the right thing, making the right decisions, and protecting the baby from harm can become a constant source of stress. For many mothers, motherhood involves a delicate balance between the instinct to protect and the need to allow her child to explore and grow on her own.

One of the biggest challenges women face in motherhood is the struggle to find a balance between being a mother and maintaining their individual identity. Motherhood requires immense dedication, but that doesn't mean a woman should lose herself in the process. Many women struggle with feelings of guilt when trying to balance caring for their children with attending to their own needs, interests, and careers. However, it is important to remember that self-care and self-expression are not only vital to the mother's well-being, but also benefit the child. A mother who feels fulfilled and balanced is better able to care for her child and teach him the value of balance in life.

Society also plays an important role in the experience of motherhood. Cultural and social expectations can strongly influence how a woman feels and views herself as a mother. Mothers are often expected to be perfect, always available, patient and loving at all times. These expectations can be a heavy burden, especially in an era where idealized images of motherhood are everywhere, from social media to advertising. Mothers may feel pressured to meet an unattainable ideal, which can lead to frustration, guilt, and a feeling of not being good enough.

Another important aspect of motherhood is social support. Motherhood can be an isolating experience if a woman does not have the right support. Support networks, whether family, friends, or mothers' groups, are essential to helping women navigate the challenges of motherhood. Sharing experiences, asking for advice, and simply having someone to talk to can make a big difference in how a mother feels and handles her new life. Additionally, partner support is crucial. Co-parenting not only eases the burden on the mother, but also strengthens the family bond and promotes a more balanced and harmonious environment for the child.

Motherhood can also be a time of personal growth and development. Many women discover new strengths and abilities in themselves that they have never known before. Patience, empathy, the ability to love unconditionally, and the ability to handle multiple responsibilities at once are just some of the qualities that motherhood can develop. This personal growth not only enriches the mother's life, but also provides her with valuable tools to face other aspects of life.

However, it is important to recognize that motherhood is not always an easy or pleasant experience. Some women face significant challenges, such as postpartum depression, which can make the transition to motherhood especially difficult. Postpartum depression is a serious condition that affects many women and is often characterized by feelings of deep sadness, extreme fatigue, and difficulty connecting with the baby. It is crucial that women experiencing these symptoms seek help, as postpartum depression is treatable and the right support can make a big difference in recovery.

In short, motherhood is a rich, multifaceted experience that profoundly transforms a woman's life. It is a journey full of love, responsibility, challenges and growth. Although each woman experiences motherhood in a unique way, there are common elements that they all share, from the emotional bond with her child to the pressures and expectations they face. Understanding and supporting women on their journey as mothers is essential not only for their well-being, but also for the well-being of future generations. Motherhood is one of the most powerful and significant experiences a woman can live, and deserves to be celebrated and respected in all its complexity.

Gerard Roussel

Self-image and Body Perception

Self-image and body perception are deeply rooted issues in a woman's life. From a young age, women are bombarded with messages about how they should look, what is considered beautiful, and how their bodies should fit certain social standards. These messages can come from family, friends, the media and, increasingly, social networks. As women grow, these standards often become internalized, shaping how they see themselves and how they perceive their bodies. Self-image and body perception can influence almost every aspect of a woman's life, from her self-esteem to her relationships, and it is crucial to understand how they develop and how they can be transformed.

Self-image is the way a woman sees herself, both physically and emotionally. It is influenced by a combination of internal and external factors, including personal experiences, relationships, and cultural norms. Body perception, on the other hand, refers specifically to how a woman sees and feels her body. This includes your size, shape, weight, and physical characteristics such as hair, skin, and facial features. For many women, self-image and body perception are intrinsically intertwined. When a woman has a positive self-image, she tends to feel good about her body and vice versa. However, if a woman has a negative perception of her body, it is likely to affect her overall self-image.

One of the most powerful factors that influences self-image and body perception is social comparison. Women often compare themselves to others, whether to friends, celebrities, or even idealized images they see in advertising. This comparison can be devastating, as it is often based on unattainable and unrealistic ideals. Images of perfect bodies seen in the media are often airbrushed and do not represent reality. However, many women feel pressure to achieve these ideals, which can lead to body dissatisfaction and low self-esteem. It's easy to fall into the trap of thinking that to be valued or loved, a woman must have a body that fits certain standards, but this mentality is destructive and false.

The impact of a negative body perception can be profound. Women who are unhappy with their bodies may experience a variety of negative emotions, such as shame, anxiety, and sadness. These emotions can lead to unhealthy behaviors, such as extreme dieting, excessive exercise, or even eating disorders. Additionally, body dissatisfaction can affect a woman's confidence in her daily life. She may feel less confident in social situations, avoid certain activities, or even turn down professional opportunities because she is not comfortable with the way she looks. In short, negative body perception can severely limit a woman's potential and her ability to enjoy life.

However, it is important to recognize that body perception is not fixed. Women can work to change the way they see themselves and their bodies. This is not an easy or quick process, but it is possible. A key approach is learning to challenge negative thoughts and irrational beliefs about the body. Instead of focusing on what they perceive as flaws, women can learn to appreciate their bodies for what they are and what they can do. This includes recognizing that all bodies are different and that there is no perfect body. Beauty comes in all shapes, sizes and colors, and every woman has something unique and valuable to offer.

Another important strategy to improve body perception is to practice self-care and acceptance. Self-care means treating your body with respect and care, including healthy eating, regular exercise, and adequate rest. It also means treating yourself with kindness and compassion, rather than constantly criticizing yourself. Acceptance, on the other hand, involves recognizing that the body changes over time and that these changes are a natural part of life. This can be especially challenging in a culture that values youth and thinness, but learning to accept one's body as it is can free women from the pressure of meeting impossible standards.

The role of community and social support is also crucial in forming a healthy body perception. Women who surround themselves with people who support them and value them for who they are, rather than how they look, tend to have better body perception. Friendships and family relationships that foster acceptance and self-love are essential. Additionally, participating in communities that promote body diversity and inclusion can help women see beauty in all its forms and feel less pressure to conform to a single ideal.

Social media, while often a contributing factor to body dissatisfaction, can also be a positive tool if used consciously. By following accounts and people that promote body-positive messages, and staying away from those that encourage unrealistic comparisons, women can create a digital environment that supports a healthy self-image. Additionally, being aware of how one uses social media and limiting the time spent comparing oneself to others can make a big difference in how a woman feels about her body.

Self-image and body perception are also influenced by the stage of life a woman is in. During adolescence, when the body changes rapidly, many young women struggle to adapt to their new appearance. The pressure to fit in and be accepted by peers can be intense, which can seriously affect body perception. In adulthood, women may face new challenges, such as bodily changes related to pregnancy, aging, or menopause. Each of these stages brings with it unique challenges, but also opportunities to learn to love and accept your body in new ways.

It is important to remember that self-image and body perception not only affect women individually, but also have an impact on society as a whole. When women feel confident and satisfied with their bodies, they are better equipped to fully participate in life, take risks, and pursue their goals. A society where women feel valued for who they are rather than how they look is a more just and equitable society. Promoting positive body perception is not only a matter of personal well-being, but also of social justice.

Ultimately, self-image and body perception are essential aspects of a woman's overall well-being. Learning to accept and love your body as it is can be challenging, but it is a crucial step toward a fuller, happier life. By challenging unrealistic beauty ideals, practicing self-care, and surrounding themselves with a supportive community, women can transform their body perception and develop a self-image that reflects their true value. Real beauty is not in meeting an external standard, but in the confidence, strength and authenticity that emanates from a woman who feels good about herself.

Women and Sexuality

Sexuality is a fundamental part of a woman's identity, deeply influencing how she feels about herself, how she relates to others, and how she experiences life. However, despite its importance, female sexuality has long been a topic surrounded by taboos, misunderstandings, and cultural expectations that can leave women feeling confused or even repressed about their own desire and pleasure. Talking openly about female sexuality is essential so that women can better understand themselves, feel empowered in their relationships, and enjoy a full and healthy sex life.

Female sexuality is much more than mere biological function. It involves a combination of physical, emotional, psychological and social factors. From a biological perspective, sexuality is related to sexual desire, arousal, and the body's physiological response. However, the experience of sexuality is unique to each woman and is influenced by her personal history, her beliefs, her past experiences, and the cultural and social norms that surround her. Sexuality is often intertwined with self-esteem and self-image;

How a woman feels about her body can profoundly affect her willingness and ability to enjoy sex.

One of the most important aspects of female sexuality is the right to experience and enjoy pleasure. For a long time, society has promoted the idea that sexual pleasure is secondary for women, or that their sexuality should be at the service of their partners' satisfaction. However, pleasure is a natural and healthy part of a woman's sex life. The right to pleasure includes not only the ability to enjoy sex, but also the freedom to explore your own sexuality without shame or guilt. This implies that women have the right to know their bodies, to express their desires, and to seek pleasure in a way that makes them feel comfortable and respected.

Sexuality education is a crucial component for women to understand and feel comfortable with their sexuality. Without proper education, many women grow up with erroneous or incomplete ideas about sex, which can lead to confusion or fear.

Sexual education must cover not only the biology of the body, but also aspects such as consent, communication in sexual relations, and the importance of pleasure. Additionally, it is important that sexuality education includes a positive and respectful perspective on sexuality, helping women feel empowered rather than ashamed.

Communication is another essential pillar in female sexuality. For many women, talking openly about their sexual desires and needs can be difficult, whether because of shame, fear of rejection, or simply because they have not been educated to do so. However, communication is key to a satisfying sex life. Women should feel safe to express what they like, what they don't like, and what they need in a sexual relationship. This communication not only improves the quality of sex, but also strengthens intimacy and trust in the relationship.

Sexual relationships are influenced by a series of emotional and psychological factors. Self-esteem, for example, plays a crucial role in how a woman feels during sex.

If a woman feels confident in herself and her body, she is more likely to enjoy sex and feel comfortable exploring her sexuality. Conversely, if a woman struggles with low self-esteem or has a negative perception of her body, she may feel inhibited or less willing to engage in sexual activities. That's why working on self-esteem and self-acceptance is so important for a healthy sex life.

Past experiences can also have a big impact on a woman's sexuality. Women who have had negative experiences, such as sexual abuse or toxic relationships, may find that these experiences affect their ability to enjoy sex or trust a partner. It is essential that these women receive the appropriate support to heal and reclaim their sexuality in a way that is healthy and empowering. Therapy, support from loved ones, and positive sexuality education can be valuable tools in overcoming these challenges.

Culture and society also play a significant role in female sexuality. Cultural expectations about how a woman "should" behave sexually can influence how a woman feels about her sexuality. In many cultures, women face double pressure: on the one hand, they are told to be reserved and modest, while on the other hand, they are required to be attractive and sexually available. These conflicting expectations can lead to confusion and stress, and can make it difficult for women to feel free to explore and enjoy their sexuality on their own terms.

Furthermore, female sexuality is not static; changes throughout life. As a woman goes through different stages, such as adolescence, young adulthood, pregnancy, motherhood, and menopause, her sexuality also evolves. These changes are natural and reflect the dynamic nature of a woman's sex life. It is important that women feel comfortable with these changes and understand that each stage brings with it new experiences and opportunities for sexual growth.

One of the challenges that many women face in their sexuality is the myth that they must meet certain performance or appearance standards to be desirable or enjoy sex. These myths can be harmful and create unnecessary pressure, leading to a disconnection from your own desire and pleasure. It is crucial that women free themselves from these expectations and understand that sexuality is a personal and unique experience, which does not need to conform to any external standards. True sexual pleasure comes from being present in the moment, being in tune with one's body, and enjoying an intimate connection with a partner.

Consent is another fundamental aspect of female sexuality. Consent means that all parties involved in a sexual relationship must clearly and enthusiastically agree to engage in sexual activity. Consent is not just a matter of saying "yes" or "no"; It also involves continuous communication and respect for each person's boundaries. Consent ensures that all sexual experiences are safe, respectful, and pleasurable for all parties involved. Teaching and practicing consent is crucial for women to feel safe and empowered in their sex lives.

Ultimately, female sexuality is an essential part of what it means to be a woman. It is a source of pleasure, connection, and personal power. For many women, embracing their sexuality is a path to greater self-understanding and self-acceptance. However, to achieve healthy and satisfying sexuality, it is necessary to break the myths and taboos that have surrounded female sexuality for so long. By talking openly about sex, educating themselves, and communicating with their partners, women can reclaim their sexuality as a natural and beautiful part of who they are. Female sexuality is not something to be feared or repressed; It is a source of strength, joy and connection that deserves to be celebrated and respected in all its complexity and diversity.

Feminine Resilience

Feminine resilience is the ability of women to face, overcome and grow from the adversities and challenges they encounter in life. Throughout history, women have demonstrated a remarkable ability to adapt to difficult circumstances, find strength in moments of weakness, and move forward despite obstacles. Resilience is not just an innate characteristic, but a skill that can be cultivated and strengthened over time. Understanding and developing resilience is essential for women to navigate life's difficulties and find personal satisfaction.

Female resilience is not an abstract concept; It manifests itself in the daily lives of women. It can be seen in the single mother who, despite her financial difficulties, manages to raise her children with love and dedication. It is found in the woman who, after a serious illness, finds the courage to start over and rebuild her life. It is also present in the woman who, faced with discrimination or harassment in the workplace, moves forward with determination, fighting for her place and her voice. These examples are just a small sample of how resilience is expressed in the lives of millions of women around the world.

A key component of resilience is the ability to adapt to change. Life is full of transitions, some desired and others imposed by circumstances beyond our control. Women often face significant changes in their lives, such as starting a career, motherhood, caring for sick family members, or the loss of a loved one. Each of these changes requires adaptation, and resilience allows women to find new ways to live and thrive, even in the midst of uncertainty. Adapting does not mean simply accepting what comes, but finding ways to thrive in new circumstances.

Another important aspect of resilience is the ability to maintain a positive outlook even in difficult situations. This doesn't mean ignoring pain or difficulty, but finding the courage to look beyond them and look for opportunities for growth. Resilient women tend to focus on what they can control instead of obsessing about what they can't. They also look for meaning and lessons in difficult experiences, using those lessons to strengthen themselves and move forward. This positive outlook can be a powerful source of motivation and energy, helping women keep going when things get tough.

Social support is a crucial factor in female resilience. Relationships with friends, family, and colleagues can provide invaluable emotional sustenance during difficult times. When women face challenges, having a support network can make the difference between feeling overwhelmed and finding the strength to keep going. This support not only offers comfort, but can also provide new perspectives and solutions to problems. Resilient women are not afraid to ask for help when they need it, recognizing that strength is also found in the ability to accept support from others.

Resilience also involves the ability to learn and grow from adversity. Resilient women not only survive hardships, but often emerge from them stronger and wiser. They see difficult experiences as opportunities to learn more about themselves, develop new skills, and strengthen their character. This growth mindset allows women to transform difficulties into catalysts for positive change. Instead of being defined by their challenges, resilient women are defined by how they respond to them and how they use those experiences to improve their lives.

Self-care is another essential component of resilience. In order to face life's challenges, women need to take care of their physical, emotional and mental well-being. This includes making sure they are getting enough rest, eating properly, and finding time for activities that rejuvenate them and bring them joy. Self-care is not a luxury; It is a fundamental need that allows women to maintain the strength and energy necessary to face adversity. Additionally, self-care includes practicing self-compassion, treating yourself with kindness and understanding, especially in times of difficulty.

Female resilience is also deeply connected to self-determination. Women who are resilient tend to have a strong sense of purpose and direction in life. They know what they want and are willing to work for it, even when they face obstacles. This self-determination gives them the energy and persistence to keep going, even when times are tough. Resilience does not mean never falling; It means having the strength and determination to get up again and again, no matter how many times life knocks you down.

Furthermore, female resilience is enhanced by women's ability to find and nurture hope. Hope is not just a feeling, but a powerful force that drives women to continue fighting, even in the most desperate situations. Hope allows women to see a better future, even when the present is bleak, and gives them the motivation to keep going. Resilient women keep hope alive, knowing that, although the road may be difficult, there is always a possibility for improvement and growth.

Resilience also involves the ability to forgive and let go. Sometimes women face deep wounds, whether from personal betrayals, injustices, or painful losses. Resilience does not require forgetting what has happened, but it does invite women to release the weight of resentment and anger in order to move forward. Forgiveness, both towards others and towards oneself, is a powerful act that allows women to heal and free themselves from the emotional chains that can impede their growth.

Finally, it is important to recognize that female resilience is not a permanent state or fixed trait. It is a dynamic capability that can be strengthened with time and experience. Each challenge faced and overcome adds a new layer of strength, allowing women to face future challenges with greater confidence and skill. Resilience is a continuous process of learning, adaptation and growth that accompanies women throughout their lives.

In conclusion, feminine resilience is a powerful force that allows women to face life's adversities with courage, wisdom and grace. It is not about being invulnerable, but about finding within themselves the strength to get up after each fall, learn from each experience and move forward with determination. Resilience is a reflection of women's innate ability to adapt, grow and thrive, even in the darkest of times. By cultivating this resilience, women not only strengthen themselves, but also inspire those around them, proving that despite challenges, there is always a path to improvement and success.

Gerard Roussel

Self-care as a Psychological Tool

Self-care is an essential psychological tool that allows women to maintain their physical, emotional and mental well-being. Although it is sometimes associated with superficial acts like taking a relaxing bath or buying something nice, self-care goes far beyond those gestures. It is a continuous practice of caring for oneself holistically, attending to the deepest needs of the body and mind. In a world where demands and expectations are increasing, self-care becomes a fundamental act to preserve mental and emotional health.

At its core, self-care involves making conscious decisions to protect and improve personal well-being. This may mean setting clear boundaries, prioritizing rest, maintaining a healthy diet, or finding time for activities that bring joy and satisfaction. Self-care is not a luxury or a selfish act; It is a vital need that allows women to be at their best, both for themselves and for those around them. When a woman takes care of herself, she is not only investing in her well-being, but she is also building the foundation upon which she can face life's challenges with greater strength and resilience.

One of the most important aspects of self-care is stress management. In modern life, stress is an inevitable reality, but how that stress is managed can make a big difference in mental and emotional health. Women who practice self-care learn to recognize early signs of stress and take steps to mitigate it before it becomes overwhelming. This may include relaxation techniques such as meditation, deep breathing, or simply taking some time to disconnect from daily responsibilities and recharge. Self-care also involves being aware of your own emotions and giving them the space they need to be processed in a healthy way.

Self-care also manifests in women's ability to set and maintain healthy boundaries. Boundaries are essential to protect emotional well-being and avoid burnout. Many times, women can feel pressured to say yes to everything, whether out of fear of disappointing others or a belief that they should be able to handle it all. However, learning to say no when necessary is a powerful act of self-care. By setting clear boundaries, women ensure that they are prioritizing their well-being and that they have the energy and time to properly care for themselves.

Another key component of self-care is maintaining a social support network. Relationships with friends, family, and coworkers can be an invaluable source of emotional strength. Sharing experiences, seeking advice, or simply spending time with people who care about us can be extremely comforting and restorative. Self-care involves recognizing the importance of these relationships and making a conscious effort to nurture them. It also means being selective about relationships, choosing to surround yourself with people who contribute positively to well-being and avoiding those who can be toxic or draining.

Diet and exercise are fundamental aspects of physical self-care that also have a significant impact on psychological well-being. Eating a balanced, nutrient-dense diet is not only essential for physical health, but it also has a direct impact on mood and energy. Likewise, regular exercise is one of the most effective ways to reduce stress, improve mood, and increase self-esteem. Self-care involves integrating healthy habits into your daily routine, not as an obligation, but as a way to nourish the body and mind so they can function at their best.

Sleep is another crucial pillar of self-care. Lack of sleep can have devastating effects on mental health, affecting mood, concentration and the ability to manage stress. Despite this, many women underestimate the importance of adequate rest, often sacrificing hours of sleep to fulfill their multiple responsibilities. Self-care involves prioritizing sleep, recognizing that it is as essential as any other activity in your daily routine. Establishing a regular sleep routine, creating an environment conducive to rest, and avoiding the use of electronic devices before bed are important steps to ensure restful sleep.

Self-care also includes the practice of self-compassion, which is the ability to treat yourself with kindness and understanding, especially in times of difficulty. Many women are their own worst critics, judging themselves harshly for their mistakes or imperfections. However, self-compassion involves recognizing that all people make mistakes and that it is natural to have weaknesses. By practicing self-compassion, women can relieve the internal pressure they place on themselves and approach their challenges with greater patience and kindness. This not only reduces stress, but also strengthens self-esteem and emotional well-being.

Additionally, self-care encompasses the search for meaning and purpose in life. Women who feel connected to a larger purpose, whether through their work, their relationships, or their passions, tend to have greater personal satisfaction and resilience. Self-care involves taking time to explore and cultivate these areas of meaning. This may include finding time for hobbies that bring joy, engaging in activities that contribute to the well-being of others, or simply reflecting on what really matters in life. By nurturing a sense of purpose, women strengthen their emotional well-being and find an internal source of motivation and satisfaction.

Time management is another essential aspect of self-care. In a life full of responsibilities and commitments, it is easy to feel overwhelmed by a lack of time. Self-care involves learning to manage time effectively, establishing clear priorities and avoiding overload. This may include delegating tasks, learning to say no, and making sure enough time is spent on activities that really matter. Time management also involves leaving room for rest and recreation, recognizing that these are essential components of a balanced and healthy lifestyle.

Finally, self-care is a powerful tool for personal growth. By taking care of themselves, women not only preserve their current well-being, but also build a solid foundation for their future development. Self-care allows women to be more in tune with their needs, desires, and limits, which helps them make more informed and conscious decisions. Additionally, self-care promotes greater self-acceptance and self-confidence, empowering women to face life's challenges with greater confidence and determination.

In summary, self-care as a psychological tool is essential for the comprehensive well-being of women. It is not just sporadic acts of indulgence, but an ongoing practice of tending to physical, emotional, and mental needs. By incorporating self-care into their daily routine, women can improve their health, reduce stress, and develop greater resilience in the face of difficulties. In a world that often demands too much, self-care is a way to ensure that women stay strong, balanced and able to face any challenges life throws at them.

Toxic Relationships and Their Impact on Women

Toxic relationships can be devastating to a woman's well-being, affecting her emotional, mental, and even physical health. Often, toxic relationships don't start out in an obvious way; They can develop slowly over time, as patterns of harmful behavior become established and deepen. Understanding what a toxic relationship is, how to identify it, and, most importantly, how to protect yourself from its effects is crucial for any woman who wants to maintain her well-being and happiness.

A toxic relationship is one in which one or both people experience a persistent pattern of negative behavior that drains energy, reduces self-esteem, and creates an environment of constant stress. These behaviors can include manipulation, excessive control, excessive jealousy, constant criticism, lack of emotional support, and, in the most serious cases, physical or emotional abuse. Although toxic relationships can exist in any type of relationship—whether romantic, friendly, or family—in this chapter we will focus on toxic relationships in the romantic context, as they often have a deep and lasting impact on a woman's life.

One of the most damaging effects of a toxic relationship is the erosion of self-esteem. Women in toxic relationships often find themselves questioning their own worth and dignity. This can happen when their partner constantly criticizes them, puts them down, or makes them feel like they are never good enough. Over time, these criticisms can be internalized, leading the woman to believe that she really doesn't deserve better or that her faults are the cause of the problems in the relationship. This cycle of self-criticism and low self-esteem can trap a woman in a toxic relationship, making it difficult for her to see a way out or imagine a better life.

Toxic relationships can also deeply affect mental health. Constant stress, anxiety and depression are common among women who are trapped in these types of relationships. The uncertainty about what the next interaction with your partner will be like, the fear of triggering a negative reaction, and the constant pressure to try to avoid conflict can lead to a state of constant tension. This tension can manifest itself in physical symptoms such as headaches, fatigue, digestive problems, and difficulty sleeping. Over time, the cumulative impact of these symptoms can have serious repercussions on a woman's overall health.

In addition to the emotional and mental damage, toxic relationships can also limit opportunities for personal growth and development. In a toxic relationship, it is common for the partner to try to control or isolate the woman, limiting her access to other relationships, job opportunities, or activities that could enrich her life. This form of control can be subtle, such as criticizing the woman's friends or family, or more explicit, such as prohibiting her from seeing certain people or participating in certain activities. This restriction not only reduces a woman's freedom, but can also make her feel trapped and increasingly dependent on her toxic partner.

Social isolation is another devastating effect of toxic relationships. As a woman becomes more controlled or criticized by her partner, she may begin to distance herself from her support network, either because she feels ashamed of her situation or because her partner has criticized her. convinced that these relationships are harmful. This isolation weakens her support system and leaves her even more vulnerable to the manipulation and control of her partner. Without a strong support system, it can be difficult for a woman to see the reality of her situation and find the strength to leave the toxic relationship.

Toxic relationships can also distort the perception of what a healthy relationship is. Women who have been in a toxic relationship for a long time may come to accept abuse as normal or inevitable. They may begin to believe that all relationships are difficult or that love always involves suffering. This distortion of reality can lead them to enter new toxic relationships in the future, repeating harmful patterns because they have not had the opportunity to experience or learn what a truly healthy and supportive relationship is.

A toxic relationship also affects a woman's ability to trust others. Betrayal, deception, and emotional abuse can leave deep scars that make it difficult to open up to new relationships in the future. Even after leaving a toxic relationship, a woman may find that she has a hard time trusting other people or allowing anyone to get close to her emotionally. This lack of trust can not only limit her ability to form new relationships, but it can also affect her overall well-being, leaving her feeling isolated and disconnected from the world around her.

Recognizing that you are in a toxic relationship is the first step to regaining control over your life and well-being. However, it is not always easy to identify a toxic relationship, especially when one is emotionally involved. Signs of a toxic relationship may include constantly feeling exhausted after interacting with your partner, feeling like you can't be yourself, or experiencing increased anxiety or sadness. It is also important to pay attention to one's own emotions and thoughts: if one finds oneself constantly justifying one's partner's behavior or feeling trapped in the relationship, something is probably not right.

Getting out of a toxic relationship can be extremely difficult, but it is essential for mental and emotional health. The process may involve facing significant fears and challenges, such as the possibility of being alone or confrontation with a partner. However, it is important to remember that the freedom and well-being that comes from leaving a toxic relationship is invaluable. Regaining autonomy, self-esteem and the ability to live a full and healthy life is a goal worth pursuing.

External support is crucial during the process of getting out of a toxic relationship. Talking with friends, family, or a therapist can provide the perspective and support needed to make difficult decisions. A therapist, in particular, can help a woman understand how the toxic relationship has affected her mental and emotional health, and develop strategies to heal and rebuild her life. Support can also come from support groups, where you can share experiences and receive advice from people who have been through similar situations.

Finally, it is important to remember that leaving a toxic relationship is only the first step toward healing. Full recovery can take time and effort, as it involves rebuilding self-esteem, healing emotional wounds, and learning to trust and love again. However, over time, most women find that life outside of a toxic relationship is freer, healthier, and happier. The resilience and strength that is developed during this process not only helps overcome the pain of the past, but also prepares women to build healthier and more satisfying relationships in the future.

In conclusion, toxic relationships can have a devastating impact on a woman's life, affecting her self-esteem, mental health, and general well-being. However, it is possible to recognize these relationships, move out of them, and begin the healing process. By doing so, women can reclaim their power, their happiness, and their ability to live full and meaningful lives. Learning to identify and avoid toxic relationships is a crucial skill for any woman who wants to protect her emotional well-being and build a rich and fulfilling life.

Personal Development and Self-Realization

Personal development and self-realization are fundamental concepts for a full and satisfying life. For a woman, these processes are the key to understanding who she really is, what she wants in life and how she can reach her full potential. Throughout life, women face a series of challenges and expectations, both external and internal, that can divert their path towards personal growth. However, personal development is a powerful tool to overcome those obstacles, find purpose, and achieve a life rich in meaning.

Personal development refers to the continuous process of improving oneself, not only in terms of skills or knowledge, but also in emotional and spiritual growth. It is a journey that begins with self-awareness: the ability to look at yourself honestly and reflectively, to identify strengths and areas for improvement. Self-awareness is crucial because it allows women to recognize their true desires, aspirations and values, rather than simply following what others expect of them. This self-knowledge is the first step towards self-actualization, as it provides a solid foundation from which to make decisions that are aligned with the authentic self.

A central aspect of personal development is overcoming limiting beliefs. Throughout life, many women adopt negative beliefs about themselves, whether due to past experiences, cultural messages, or criticism from others. These limiting beliefs can act as invisible barriers that prevent growth and success. For example, a woman may believe that she is not intelligent, capable, or worthy enough to achieve her goals. However, personal development involves challenging these beliefs, critically examining them, and replacing them with more empowering thoughts. By doing so, women open up new possibilities for their lives and move one step closer to self-realization.

Goal setting is another essential component of personal development. Goals provide direction and purpose, and allow women to focus their energy on what really matters to them. It is important that these goals are realistic and achievable, but also ambitious and challenging. Setting goals that are aligned with personal values and resonate deeply with the authentic self helps maintain motivation and commitment over time. Additionally, the process of setting and achieving goals strengthens self-confidence, as each achievement reinforces the belief in one's own ability to overcome challenges and achieve success.

Personal development also involves the continuous improvement of skills and knowledge. In a rapidly changing world, the ability to learn and adapt is crucial. This can range from acquiring new professional skills to learning to better manage emotions or improving interpersonal skills. Education and learning not only increase job opportunities, but also enrich personal lives and foster a sense of achievement and satisfaction. For women, a commitment to continuous learning is a way to stay relevant and resilient, as well as a means to achieve their dreams and aspirations.

Self-actualization, on the other hand, is the process of reaching one's full potential. It is the pinnacle of personal development, where a woman has not only discovered who she is, but she has also begun to live according to that truth. Self-actualization is not a destination, but a continuous journey of growth, where each new experience and challenge offers an opportunity to learn and evolve. It is a state in which a woman feels at peace with herself, satisfied with her achievements and confident in her ability to continue growing and reaching new goals.

One of the biggest obstacles to self-realization is fear. Fear of failure, the judgment of others, or even success can paralyze a woman and prevent her from pursuing her dreams. However, personal development involves learning to manage these fears, recognizing them without letting them control decisions. Courage is not the absence of fear, but the ability to act despite it. As the women face and overcome their fears, they discover a new confidence in themselves and their ability to face any challenge that comes their way.

Personal development is also intrinsically linked to emotional and mental well-being. As a woman works on her personal growth, she learns to better manage her emotions, maintain a positive outlook, and develop resilience in the face of adversity. Emotional well-being is essential for self-actualization, as it allows a woman to remain balanced and focused on her goals, even in times of stress or difficulty. Furthermore, a healthy and balanced mind is better able to make the most of opportunities for growth and enjoy achievements.

Self-realization also has a spiritual component, although not necessarily religious. For many women, self-actualization involves finding a sense of purpose and connection to something bigger than themselves. This can mean a connection to the community, to nature, or to a purpose that transcends personal achievements. Spirituality in this context refers to a sense of inner peace and harmony with the world around us. For some women, this sense of purpose and connection is what gives them the strength to continue forward on their path of personal development, especially in times of difficulty.

Interpersonal relationships play an important role in personal development and self-realization. Women who surround themselves with people who support, inspire and motivate them are better equipped to grow and achieve their goals. Healthy relationships provide a source of emotional support and a safe space to share experiences and challenges. Additionally, being surrounded by people who share similar values and aspirations can serve as a powerful catalyst for personal growth. However, it is also important to be selective in relationships, as toxic relationships can hinder personal development and divert focus from self-actualization.

Self-care, as we mentioned in a previous chapter, is a crucial part of personal development. Without a focus on physical and emotional well-being, it is difficult to have the energy and mental clarity necessary for personal growth. Self-care is not only a way to maintain balance, but it is also a way to honor and respect one's body and mind, which in turn reinforces self-esteem and self-confidence. Practicing self-care on a regular basis allows women to stay at their best, making it easier for them to face the challenges of personal development with greater effectiveness and determination.

Self-actualization also involves accepting responsibility for one's own life. This means stopping blaming circumstances or others for what hasn't gone well, and instead taking control of decisions and actions. Personal responsibility is a vital component of growth, as it empowers women to create the life they want, rather than waiting for something or someone else to do it for them. By taking responsibility, women become the architects of their own destiny, able to shape their lives according to their true desires and aspirations.

Finally, personal development and self-realization are never-ending processes. No matter how many goals have been achieved or how many obstacles have been overcome, there is always more to discover, learn and achieve. This continuous journey of growth is what makes life rich and meaningful. As women commit to their personal development, they discover that self-actualization is not a fixed state, but rather a constant evolution toward increasingly authentic and fulfilling versions of themselves.

In conclusion, personal development and self-actualization are essential for a woman to live a life full of purpose and fulfillment. These processes require self-awareness, goal setting, overcoming fears and limiting beliefs, and a continued commitment to learning and growth. Although the path may be full of challenges, the end result is a life in which a woman feels completely fulfilled, at peace with herself, and empowered to continue growing and evolving in all areas of her life.

Women and Aging

Aging is a natural process that everyone experiences, but for many women, this process is fraught with social expectations, cultural pressures, and complex emotions. As a woman ages, she faces not only physical changes, but also transformations in her identity, her roles in life, and the way society perceives her. Understanding and accepting aging as a valuable and significant stage of life is essential so that women can live these years with grace, confidence and satisfaction.

Aging in women usually begins to manifest itself in visible physical changes. The skin loses elasticity, wrinkles appear, hair may become thinner or gray, and the body may change shape. These changes are natural and part of the life cycle, but they are often accompanied by social pressure to "age well," which for many women can mean maintaining a youthful appearance for as long as possible. This pressure can lead to feelings of insecurity and a desire to reverse or hide the signs of aging, whether through beauty products, cosmetic procedures, or lifestyle changes.

However, it is important for women to understand that beauty does not disappear with age, but rather transforms. The wisdom, experience and confidence gained over the years can add a depth and charisma that goes beyond the physical. Accepting aging means recognizing that every wrinkle tells a story, every gray hair reflects a lived experience, and that true beauty lies in the authenticity and serenity that come with maturity. Rather than fighting aging, embracing it as a natural part of the life cycle can free women from the constraints of external expectations and allow them to live with greater freedom and self-compassion.

Aging can also bring about a change in the roles a woman plays in life. The responsibilities of motherhood, work, and family care may decrease or change shape, leaving room for women to explore new opportunities and passions. This change can be both liberating and challenging. For some women, it can be a time of rediscovery, where they find themselves with more time and freedom to pursue activities they couldn't explore before. For others, the change may bring a sense of loss, especially if their identity was closely tied to these roles.

Transitioning to new stages of life can also bring reflections on meaning and purpose. As women age, they often become more introspective, evaluating what really matters to them and looking for ways to leave a positive legacy. This sense of purpose can be found in various areas, such as volunteering, mentoring, creativity, or simply enjoying everyday life in a more conscious way. For many women, this stage of life offers the opportunity to reconnect with what they are passionate about and to live more authentically, without the pressures that often accompany the younger years.

However, aging can also bring with it emotional and psychological challenges. The idea of losing youth and vitality can be difficult to accept, and for some women, the aging process may be accompanied by feelings of anxiety, depression or fear. These feelings are often amplified by a society that values youth and which can make older women feel invisible or belittled. It is crucial that women give themselves permission to feel and process these emotions, seeking support if necessary, whether through friends, family or mental health professionals.

Aging also has an impact on relationships. Dynamics with partners, children, and friends can change, and as a woman ages, she may face the loss of loved ones or loneliness. However, this stage of life can also be an opportunity to strengthen existing relationships and build new connections. Many women find that as they age, their relationships become deeper and more meaningful, based on mutual respect and a deeper understanding of themselves and others. This is a time to cultivate emotional intimacy and enjoy relationships on a more authentic and meaningful level.

In terms of health, aging brings with it the need to pay greater attention to the body. Hormonal changes, such as menopause, can have a significant impact on a woman's physical and emotional well-being. It is essential that women stay informed and seek appropriate care to manage these changes. Adopting a healthy lifestyle, including a balanced diet, regular exercise and good stress management, can help mitigate some of the negative effects of aging and promote healthy aging. Staying active and committed to your own health is a way to take control of the aging process and ensure that you live the best life possible.

Menopause, in particular, is a major milestone in a woman's life and can bring with it a number of physical and emotional changes. Some women experience symptoms such as hot flashes, mood swings, and sleep problems, while others go through menopause with few problems. However, menopause can also be seen as a time of renewal, a transition into a new phase of life in which women are no longer limited by fertility concerns. It is an opportunity to focus on personal well-being, developing new passions, and creating a life that reflects a woman's deepest values and desires.

In many ways, aging can be a time of liberation. Society's expectations may become less pressing, and women may feel freer to be themselves, without the pressure to meet certain standards or roles. This freedom can be empowering, allowing women to explore new opportunities, enjoy their hobbies, and live on their own terms. Instead of seeing aging as a decline, many women see it as an opportunity to grow and flourish in new ways, finding joy and meaning in every stage of life.

It is important to highlight that aging is not only an individual process, but also a social one. The way society treats older women has a significant impact on how they perceive aging. In many cultures, older women are revered for their wisdom and experience, while in others, they may be seen as less valuable or even invisible. However, as society evolves, so does the perception of aging. Increasingly, older women are reclaiming their place in the world, proving that life does not end with youth, but can be rich, vibrant and full of opportunity at any age.

The perception of aging is also changing in the media and popular culture. More older women are being portrayed in important roles and their experience and wisdom is celebrated. This helps change social attitudes towards aging and inspire women to embrace this stage of life with pride and confidence. It is crucial that women see positive examples of aging, showing them that it is possible to be active, vibrant and happy at any age.

In conclusion, aging is an inevitable part of life, but how it is experienced and lived depends largely on perspective and attitude. For women, aging can be a time rich in opportunities for personal growth, self-actualization, and enjoyment of life. Accepting physical and emotional changes as a natural part of the life cycle, and finding new ways to flourish at each stage, is key to experiencing aging in a positive and satisfactory way. Ultimately, aging is not an end, but a continuation of life's journey, filled with possibilities to learn, grow, and enjoy all that life has to offer.

Towards Greater Understanding and Well-being

As we come to the end of this book, it is important to reflect on what we have learned and how we can apply this knowledge to achieve greater understanding and well-being in the lives of women. The female mind is a complex and multifaceted terrain, influenced by a variety of biological, emotional, social and cultural factors. Understanding these factors and how they interact with each other is essential to promoting lasting well-being, not only in women, but also in society at large.

Understanding the female mind begins with recognizing its uniqueness. Every woman is an individual with a unique mind and set of experiences. Although there are general trends that can be observed in terms of how women process their emotions, make decisions, or relate to others, it is crucial to remember that every woman is different. Personalizing the approach to understanding and supporting women is essential. It is not about fitting all women into a mold, but about respecting and valuing their individual differences, their stories and their perspectives.

A key aspect of well-being is self-acceptance. Many times, women are faced with external expectations that can be overwhelming. From pressure to meet certain beauty standards to expectations of performance in professional and family roles, women can feel trapped in an endless cycle of demands. Self-acceptance involves recognizing these pressures, but also learning to set limits and prioritize personal well-being. Accepting yourself as you are, with strengths and weaknesses, is a fundamental step towards a more balanced and happy life.

Self-care is another essential component to women's well-being. Taking care of yourself is not a selfish act, but a necessity to maintain physical and mental health. Self-care can take many forms, from taking time to relax and unwind, to seeking support when you feel overwhelmed or facing difficult situations. Self-care also involves nourishing the body with good nutrition, regular exercise and adequate rest, as well as nourishing the mind and spirit through activities that bring joy and personal satisfaction. Women often feel responsible for caring for others, but it is important to remember that they cannot effectively care for others if they do not care for themselves first.

The search for well-being also involves understanding one's own emotions and the ability to manage them in a healthy way. Emotions are an intrinsic part of the human experience, and for women, they can be particularly intense due to a number of hormonal, social and personal factors. Instead of seeing emotions as something that needs to be suppressed or controlled, it is more beneficial to learn to recognize them, understand their origin, and express them constructively. This may involve talking to a trusted friend, writing in a journal, or seeking therapy when necessary. Emotions are not a sign of weakness, but rather a sign of what is important and what needs to be attended to in life.

An important aspect of the pursuit of wellness is developing a strong support network. Interpersonal relationships play a crucial role in women's lives. Having friends, family and colleagues who offer emotional support, understanding and companionship can make a big difference in a woman's ability to handle life's stress and challenges. Support networks can also offer different perspectives, help solve problems, and provide a sense of belonging and connection that is vital for emotional well-being.

The role of culture in women's lives is also an important factor to consider in the search for well-being. Cultural norms can influence how women view themselves, their roles in society, and the expectations they feel they must meet. Understanding the impact of culture on women's lives is essential to being able to question and, if necessary, challenge these norms. By doing so, women can find a greater sense of freedom and authenticity in their lives, living according to their own values and desires rather than those imposed by society.

Education and self-knowledge are powerful tools in the search for well-being. The more women know about their own psychology, the more able they will be to handle the challenges they face. Education in areas such as emotional intelligence, resilience, effective communication and stress management can empower women to take control of their lives and face adversity with confidence. Education also allows women to be self-advocates, advocating for their rights and needs in all areas of life.

Resilience is another key characteristic that can help women navigate life's ups and downs more easily. Resilience does not mean avoiding problems or not feeling pain, but rather the ability to bounce back after difficulties. Women who develop resilience can face challenges with a positive attitude, learn from their experiences and move forward with determination. Resilience is also related to the ability to see change as an opportunity for growth, rather than a threat. Through resilience, women can build more fulfilling and meaningful lives, no matter the circumstances.

Ultimately, the pursuit of wellness for women is an ongoing journey. There is no magic formula that works for everyone, but there are principles and practices that can guide every woman toward a fuller, more satisfying life. These include self-acceptance, self-care, emotional understanding, developing support networks, continuing education, resilience, and questioning cultural norms. By integrating these elements into daily life, women can find greater inner peace, a sense of purpose, and true satisfaction in their lives.

Wellbeing is not a static state, but a dynamic process of growth and adaptation. As life circumstances change, women must be willing to adjust their approaches and find new ways to care for themselves and others. This may involve adopting new self-care practices, reevaluating relationships and commitments, and finding new sources of support and joy. Wellness is a balance between the demands of life and personal needs, and each woman has the ability to find that balance in a way that works best for her.

Understanding the female mind is an essential first step towards well-being. By exploring and understanding the factors that influence women's thinking, emotions and behavior, it is possible to make more informed and conscious decisions in everyday life. This knowledge allows women to recognize their needs, set healthy boundaries, and seek support when necessary. By doing so, they can build a life that is not only functional, but also rich in meaning and satisfaction.

As we close this chapter, it is important to remember that the path to greater understanding and well-being is personal and unique for each woman. There is no single right path, and what works for one person may not work for another. However, by adopting an attitude of openness, curiosity and self-acceptance, each woman can find her own path to a fuller and more satisfying life. The key is to listen to your own mind and body, learn from experiences and be willing to make changes when necessary. Over time, this approach can lead to a life rich in well-being, satisfaction, and happiness.